Slimy • Scaly • Deadly
Reptiles and Amphibians

NONVENOMOUS SNAKES

D0123660

Gareth Stevens
Publishing

Please visit our Web site www.garethstevens.com. For a free color catalog of all our high-quality books, call toll free 1-800-542-2595 or fax 1-877-542-2596.

Library of Congress Cataloging-in-Publication Data
Nonvenomous snakes / Tim Harris, editor.
    p. cm. -- (Slimy, scaly, deadly reptiles and amphibians)
    Includes index.
    ISBN 978-1-4339-3432-2 (library binding) -- ISBN 978-1-4339-3433-9 (pbk.)
    ISBN 978-1-4339-3434-6 (6-pack)
    1. Snakes--Juvenile literature. I. Harris, Tim.
    QL666.O6N66 2010
    597.96--dc22   2009039216

Published in 2010 by
Gareth Stevens Publishing
111 East 14th Street, Suite 349
New York, NY 10003

© 2010 The Brown Reference Group Ltd.

For Gareth Stevens Publishing:
Art Direction: Haley Harasymiw
Editorial Direction: Kerri O'Donnell

For The Brown Reference Group Ltd:
Editorial Director: Lindsey Lowe
Managing Editor: Tim Harris
Children's Publisher: Anne O'Daly
Design Manager: David Poole
Designer: Sarah Williams
Production Director: Alastair Gourlay
Picture Researcher: Clare Newman

Picture Credits:
Front Cover: Shutterstock: Eric Isselee, Shutterstock: Maxim Petrichuk.

Creatas: 4, 17t; JI Unlimited: 5t, 11, 15b, 21c, 22t; Shutterstock: John Bell 18cl, 18br, 29t, GSK 13t, Anastasiya Igolkina 5b, Joel Kempson 27t, Timothy Craig Lubcke 28b, Michael Lynch 8, Vladimir Mucibabic 25t, Govert Nieuwland 23b, Danny Reed 14b, Sherianne Talon 16b, Morozova Tatyana 17b, Nicola Vernizzi 25b, Ayesha Wilson 19b, Sharyn Young 24c, Tim Zurowski 29b.

All Illustrations © The Brown Reference Group plc

Publisher's note to educators and parents: Our editors have carefully reviewed the Web sites that appear on p. 31 to ensure that they are suitable for students. Many Web sites change frequently, however, and we cannot guarantee that a site's future contents will continue to meet our high standards of quality and educational value. Be advised that students should be closely supervised whenever they access the Internet.

All rights reserved. No part of this book may be reproduced, stored in a retrieval system, or transmitted in any form or by any means, electronic, mechanical, photocopying, recording, or otherwise, without the prior written permission of the copyright holder.

Manufactured in the United States of America
1 2 3 4 5 6 7 8 9   12 11 10

CPSIA compliance information: Batch #BRW0102GS: For further information contact Gareth Stevens, New York, New York at 1-800-542-2595.

Contents

How often does a boa constrictor eat?

A boa eats a rat.

A boa constrictor is a large snake that lives in South America. This species squeezes its prey to death. Boas usually eat small victims, such as rats and birds, but a big boa could kill and eat a sheep. Boas are cold-blooded: they don't have to use energy from food to warm their bodies. As a result, they don't need to eat much to stay alive. A typical boa will have only four or five meals a week.

Do you know...?

Giant snakes, like pythons, use their energy very efficiently. They can survive on just a few very large meals a year!

What is the world's heaviest snake?

A green anaconda wrapped around a branch

The world's heaviest—and largest—snake is the green anaconda of South America. It is usually only female anacondas that grow to be giants. They can reach more than 33 feet (10 m) in length and weigh a quarter of a ton (250 kg). The males grow to less than a third of this size. Anacondas live in wetlands and alongside rivers flowing through tropical rain forests. The snakes are close relatives of boas, and they kill by squeezing their prey to death. The largest anacondas hunt alligators and deer.

Do you know...?

Everyone knows that snakes do not have legs, right? Well, that is not always true. Anacondas and similar large snakes, such as pythons, have tiny back legs. They are so tiny that they look more like claws sticking out of the side of the body. Male anacondas use their tiny legs to tickle females when they try to get them to mate.

Why do thread snakes live in owls' nests?

Thread snakes are very small, thin snakes. They spend most of their time burrowing in soil, where they hunt insects. It isn't surprising that they are often mistaken for worms. Even screech owls make this mistake. They carry the wormlike Texas thread snake to their nests to feed their young. Every now and then a snake wriggles free and sets up home in an owl's nest. The snakes survive by eating the insects that live in the nest. Many of these insects attack baby owls. So, the baby owls usually grow faster if their nest is being cleaned by a snake.

Do you know...?

The world's smallest snake is the lesser Antillean thread snake. This tiny reptile lives on the island of Barbados. It never grows more than about 2 inches (5 cm) long, and it is narrow enough to slither through a hole the size of a pencil lead. Like other thread snakes, this species burrows through the ground and hunts tiny ants and termites.

A Texas thread snake

What is the longest snake?

A reticulated python

Do you know...?

Like other reptiles, snakes never stop growing. They grow the fastest when they are young. The snakes that live in warm areas with plenty of food will grow fastest of all. However, the growth continues even after they become adults. Eventually, the snake's growth slows down, but it never stops completely. In places where there is plenty of food, old snakes can reach amazing lengths.

Reticulated pythons have been known to grow even longer than giant green anacondas. The pythons live in the jungles of Southeast Asia, where they hunt large prey, such as wild pigs and stray dogs. They also occasionally eat people! Most reticulated pythons grow to about 33 feet (10 m) long, but the longest was found living in Indonesia. It stretched to about 49 feet (14.9 m) long—longer than a truck!

How many lungs do snakes have?

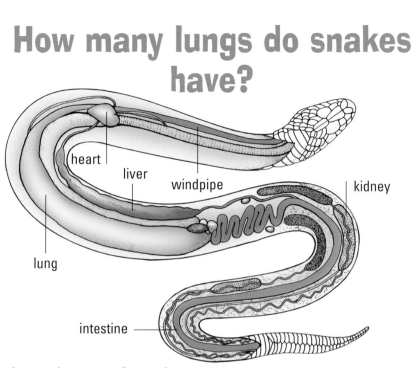

heart

liver

windpipe

kidney

lung

intestine

The internal organs of a snake

Do you know...?

Sea snakes (below) can absorb oxygen through the lining of the windpipe—the tube that links the mouth and lungs. That allows them to take in more oxygen.

Snakes have most of the same internal organs as a person. They have a heart, a liver, kidneys, and a stomach and intestines. All of these have to be packed into the snake's long, tube-shaped body—so the organs are long and thin, too. However, space is still very tight, especially when the stomach is full. Most snakes have made a little more room by having only one working lung— the right lung. The left lung is just a tiny, almost useless bag.

Do snakes have tails?

A tree snake has a long, flexible tail that it can wrap around branches.

A snake's long, wriggly body looks like one huge tail! Snakes evolved from animals that had legs. They looked a little like lizards, with four legs and a long tail. When scientists look at a snake's skeleton, they can see the shoulder and hip bones where the legs would once have been attached to the body. The tail is the bit that comes after the hip bones. Some snakes have a long, bendy tail. Others have a short, stubby one.

Do you know...?

The easiest way to see where a snake's tail begins is to find the snake's cloaca. The cloaca is an opening on the underside of the snake. The word *cloaca* means "drain" in Latin, and that is exactly what the opening is. The cloaca is the snake's only rear opening. All its waste products come out of this opening.

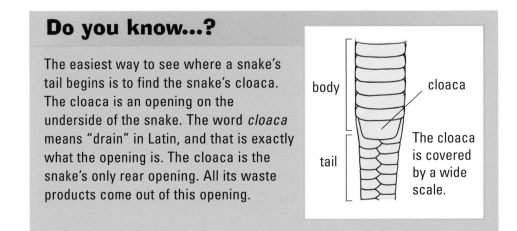

body

cloaca

tail

The cloaca is covered by a wide scale.

How does a python look after its eggs?

A python spends much of its time coiled up.

After they mate, some female snakes lay a large number of eggs in a hidden nest and then slither away. The moms are nowhere near when the eggs hatch. However, python moms take more care with their eggs. Baby snakes grow quickest inside warm eggs. A female python coils her body around her mound of eggs to keep them warm. She also adds a bit of heat by sending shiverlike waves through her body. These shivers create heat inside her muscles. That heat is passed to the eggs.

Do you know...?

King cobras build a nest of leaves for their eggs. The nest has two chambers. The eggs are laid in the bottom one, and the mom coils herself into the upper one. As the eggs hatch, the mom leaves in case she gets the urge to eat her young!

How do blind snakes dig through the ground?

As their name suggests, blind snakes cannot see. They do not need to because they spend nearly all their time burrowing in soil where it is always too dark to see anything. Most of the time, blind snakes stay out of sight, moving through the soft earth in search of buried ants' nests. A blind snake's face is covered by a single scale. The scale makes the snake's head like a spade for digging in soil. Once the head has cleared a space ahead, the snake shuffles forward and starts digging again. Blind snakes have rounded bodies. This shape makes it easier for them to move in tunnels.

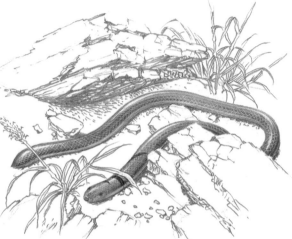

A European worm snake

Do you know...?

The shield-tailed snake is a burrowing species from Sri Lanka. It has a very unusual blunt tail, which ends in a studded shield. No one is sure what it is for, but it is probably used underground to block attacks from behind while it is in a tunnel.

How do snakes move over land?

It is surprising how many different ways snakes can move. Most snakes slither in a series of sideways curves. The body only touches the ground at the wide points of the curve. The scales on the snake's belly hook onto the ground. As the curves wave along the body, new sections grip the ground and push the snake forward. Larger snakes move using small up-and-down curves of the body, a little like a caterpillar. Burrowing snakes move more like nightcrawlers. They squeeze and stretch sections of the body in sequence so they slowly shuffle forward.

A small snake slithering

Do you know...?

Shovel-nosed snakes are sand swimmers. They use their pointed snouts to slither through loose sand and stones. They wriggle their bodies rapidly from side to side as if they were swimming through the ground.

13

Why do grass snakes pretend to be dead?

A grass snake

Grass snakes like water and are seldom seen far from a pond or stream. Grass snakes are not venomous. They grab prey in the mouth and swallow it alive. When a grass snake feels threatened, it rolls over and lies perfectly still with its tongue hanging out. The snake looks dead. Since most predators like to eat freshly killed meals, they usually leave the grass snake alone.

Do you know...?

Water snakes, such as water moccasins (below), can dive underwater for half an hour. But they need to return to the surface to breathe. Like crocodiles, which are distant relatives of snakes, water snakes have nostrils on the top of the head, so they can breathe while floating at the surface.

A Brahminy blind snake

Why don't Brahminy blind snakes mate?

Brahminy blind snakes are small burrowing snakes that live in southern Asia. They search the ground for ants' nests. Once they find one, the snakes have a huge feast! There is something very strange about these snakes, however—all Brahminy blind snakes are female. They lay eggs without needing to mate. No other snake reproduces in this way.

Do you know...?

Brahminy blind snakes are also known as flowerpot snakes because gardeners sometimes find them digging through the soil. The snakes have to search high and low for their insect food. They cannot eat anything else. Their mouths are too small to open very wide. They can't fit anything larger than an ant into it.

Why do file snakes have baggy skin?

File snakes can swim

The file snake is an unusual Australian snake. It is named for its scales which, unlike those of most other reptiles, do not overlap each other. Instead, they form rough bumps, which remind people of a file used to smooth fingernails. A file snake's skin looks loose and too large for the snake's body. Why is that? File snakes live in water, where they hunt fish. It isn't always easy for file snakes to slither along muddy pond beds. Their baggy skin allows them to bend their bodies into whatever shape is needed to grip onto the soggy bottom.

Do you know...?

File snakes live in Australian lakes called billabongs (below). Billabongs often dry out, so file snakes spend a lot of time doing nothing in the mud. File snakes do not often get the chance to breed. A female gives birth once about every ten years. That makes the file snake the world's slowest-breeding vertebrate.

Do garter snakes hibernate?

A group of garter snakes

Garter snakes live in colder places than any other American snake. Some live near the Great Slave Lake in northern Canada. This lake freezes over in winter. Garter snakes survive cold weather by hibernating. The snakes often gather in large numbers in underground dens. Some caves contain nearly 10,000 garter snakes in winter. The snakes huddle together to share their body warmth.

Do you know...?

Adders that live in cold parts of Europe and Asia are darker than ones that live in warmer regions. The dark color allows the snake to absorb more heat from its surroundings. In some places, adders are completely black.

Are green tree pythons always green?

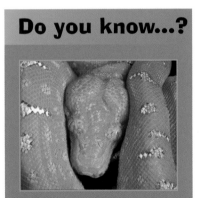

A green tree python

Adult green tree pythons are usually green. That helps them remain hidden in the trees of their forest habitat. However, young pythons are not always green when they hatch. Most are born bright yellow, but they become yellowish green, and then green, as they get older. A few tree pythons are blue throughout their lives.

Young tree pythons are yellowish green.

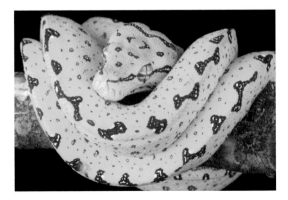

Do you know...?

Emerald tree boas are very similar to green tree pythons—but they live in different parts of the world. Like the pythons, baby tree boas are not emerald green at all—they are mostly bright orange.

A royal python coiled in a ball

How does a royal python protect itself from enemies?

Royal pythons live in some African forests. Since they are much shorter than most other pythons, they have more enemies than their bigger cousins. To defend itself from attack, a royal python wraps its body into a tight ball. Its head is somewhere in the middle of the ball and safe from attack.

Do you know...?

Royal pythons make popular pets. The snakes are not dangerous. They are smaller and easier to handle than other pythons. However, royal pythons are now rare in the wild.

How do snail-eaters kill their prey?

An American snail-eater slithers up on a snail.

Snail-eaters are small, thin snakes that live in South American rain forests. They eat snails that live on the leaves of the forest trees. A snail-eater strikes quickly, biting the snail before it can hide in its shell. The snail still retreats inside, but as it does so it pulls the snake's lower jaw into the shell with it. The upper jaw slides over the top of the shell. The teeth of the lower jaw are anchored in the snail's body. The snake then tugs the snail out of its shell.

Do you know...?

Slug snakes are similar to South American snail-eaters, but they live in Asia. Slug snakes also hunt in trees. However, the two groups are not closely related. As their name suggests, slug snakes prefer to eat slugs, but they can also tackle snails with thin shells that are easy to crack.

Why do a sunbeam snake's scales glisten?

A sunbeam snake shimmers.

Sunbeam snakes are beautiful snakes that live in Asia. They spend most of their time hunting for lizards and frogs under dead leaves. When they come out into the open, their shiny scales glisten in the light, forming a shimmering rainbow effect. The snakes' scales are covered by a see-through layer. Some light reflects off this top layer, while the rest bounces off the scales underneath. These two sets of reflections mix to make the shimmering lights.

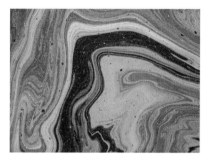

A sunbeam snake's coloring is created in the same way that patterns form on spilled oil.

Do you know...?

Sunbeam snakes have hinged teeth that they can fold backward but not forward. This helps the snake keep hold of food as it moves into the throat. The teeth make it impossible for struggling prey to escape out of the snake's mouth.

What shape are a snake's eggs?

Many snakes lay narrow, oval eggs.

Everyone knows what a chicken's egg looks like. But reptile eggs—and that includes snakes—don't look like those laid by birds. Lizards and turtles produce round eggs. Some large snakes do that, too. However, most types of snakes can't fit round eggs inside their long bodies. They produce longer, thinner eggs, which fit better inside the body. If the baby snakes have a good supply of food to eat when they hatch, they can hatch when they are only small. That means the eggs they hatch from can be small, too.

Do you know...?

The massasauga is a small American rattlesnake. It takes a long time to produce eggs. The adults mate in fall, but a female does not lay her eggs until spring.

A brown house snake

What is the most common snake in Africa?

Snakes are a common sight in many parts of Africa. People like to see some snakes more than others. For example, no one likes meeting a black mamba. This bad-tempered snake has a deadly bite. However, most people are happy to see a brown house snake. House snakes live in many parts of Africa. This medium-sized snake often slithers into people's homes. House snakes are welcomed by people because they kill mice and other pests. The snakes kill the pests by constriction, squeezing them to death.

Do you know...?

The brown house snake lives in many areas of Africa south of the Sahara Desert. Some of these snakes also live north of this desert in the Atlas Mountains of Morocco.

How do male carpet pythons find mates?

Do you know...?

After she has mated, a female python starts to grow eggs inside her body. She looks for a sunny spot in which to bask. The extra heat makes the eggs grow faster. Once she lays her eggs, the python protects them from monitor lizards.

Carpet pythons are large snakes that live in Australia. They are sometimes called diamond pythons because of the pattern some of the snakes have. Carpet pythons sleep in caves and old buildings when the weather is cold. In spring, they head for woodlands. This is the breeding season, and male carpet pythons patrol the woods looking for females. The females that are ready to mate give out a scent that the males can follow.

Each year there are many more males wanting to mate than females. Several males chase each female, and they all mate with her before looking for another female.

A carpet python

How do snakes hear without ears?

A snake's ears are hidden inside its head.

Do you know...?

The very first snakes lived underground and did not have very good eyesight. The eyes of modern snakes work better. Snake eyes still can't see things in detail, but they can pick up the movements of prey.

Snakes do not have outer ears, the parts that stick out of the sides of the head. Sounds reach their inner ears through holes in the sides of the snakes' heads. In most snakes, this hole is covered by scales. The scales block out some of the sound, so snakes' ears are not very sensitive. This is not a problem, though—snakes also pick up sounds through their jawbones. They detect vibrations running through the ground.

How do snakes squeeze their prey to death?

Snakes that squeeze their prey to death are called constrictors. The most powerful constrictors are pythons and boas. They are big snakes that coil their bodies tightly around a victim so it cannot escape. Then, the constrictors suffocate their prey. At first, the prey tries to struggle free. But moving around actually helps the snake to tighten its grip. Eventually the prey cannot move at all. Every time it breathes out, the snake tightens its grip a little more. The grip becomes so tight that the prey can't breathe in. Without air, the prey dies.

A rainbow boa is a type of constrictor.

Do you know...?

The rubber boa is a small constricting snake that lives in western North America. It is only 1 foot (30 cm) long. Its tube-shaped body is covered in shiny scales. The boa is named for the rubbery feel of these soft scales.

Can snakes chew?

A snake swallows its prey whole.

To chew, an animal needs jaws that can move sideways as well as up and down. The extra motion lets the jaw grind food into a paste that is easy to swallow. A snake's jaw can't chew, so snakes must swallow food whole. Often, prey is larger than the snake's head, but that is no problem. The upper part of a snake's jaw detaches from the lower part to make space for large meals to pass through.

Do you know...?

The egg-eating snake swallows eggs whole. It eats only freshly laid eggs and must select eggs that will fit in its mouth. Young snakes can choke on big eggs. The egg cracks in the stomach, and the snake spits out the shell.

How do snakes detect heat?

Do you know...?

Black-headed pythons do not have heat-sensitive pits because they eat cold-blooded prey. The victims are not hotter than their surroundings, so pits would not be able to detect them.

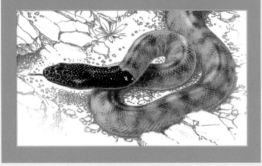

Pythons, boas, and many vipers are able to "see" heat by using heat detectors on their snouts. The detectors are shallow holes, or pits. Each pit has a heat-sensitive lining, which can feel the warmth given off by a warm-blooded animal. The pits are sensitive enough for a snake to find prey in total darkness. Sometimes, the victim of a snake's bite scurries away after being bitten. The snake needs to wait for the animal to die, then tracks down the warmth of its body.

A python has heat-sensitive pits on its snout.

Do snakes have cold blood?

A rattlesnake sunbathes.

Snakes and other reptiles are cold-blooded animals. This does not mean that the animals' blood is chilled. Warm-blooded animals keep their bodies at a steady temperature, usually warmer than the air. The temperature of a cold-blooded snake, on the other hand, goes up and down with the temperature of its surroundings. On cold days, a snake can only move slowly because its cold muscles don't work well. On a warm day, the snake can move with lightning speed. Snakes bask in sunshine to warm their bodies before going hunting.

Do you know...?

Garter snakes live in places where it freezes every winter. The snakes have chemicals in their blood to keep it from freezing.

Glossary

bask: to lie in warm sunshine and soak up the Sun's warmth

cloaca: the opening on the underside of a snake that is used for reproduction and excretion

cold-blooded: having a body temperature that changes with the temperature of the surroundings

constrictor: a snake that squeezes its prey until it suffocates and dies

evolve: to change over a long period of time

habitat: a particular kind of environment, such as a forest or a desert

hibernate: to slow down the body processes and become inactive during cold or very dry periods

mate: to come together to produce young; either of a breeding pair of animals

predator: an animal that hunts other animals for food

prey: an animal that is hunted by another animal

reticulated: having a pattern that looks like a net

scale: a tough, waterproof plate that grows out of the skin of some reptiles

species: a group of animals that share features, and can mate and produce young together

venomous: able to produce a poisonous liquid, called venom. Many snakes are venomous. They inject the poison into their victims by biting.

vertebrate: an animal that has a backbone

warm-blooded: having a body temperature that remains constant even when the surrounding temperature changes

Find Out More

Books about nonvenomous snakes

Bredeson, Carmen. *Boa Constrictors Up Close*. Berkeley Heights, NJ: Enslow Elementary, 2006.

Clarke, Penny. *Snakes Alive.* Danbury, CT: Franklin Watts, 2002.

Frost, Helen. *Boa Constrictors*. Mankato, MN: Capstone Press, 2006.

Markle, Sandra. *Outside and Inside Snakes*. New York: Aladdin Paperbacks, 1998.

Montgomery, Sy. *The Snake Scientist*. New York, NY: Sandpiper, 2001.

Schlaepfer, Gloria G., and Mary Lou Samuelson. *Pythons and Boas*. Danbury, CT: Franklin Watts, 2002.

Useful websites

Boa Constrictor
animals.nationalgeographic.com/animals/reptiles/ boa-constrictor.html

Different Types of Snakes
www.buzzle.com/articles/different-types-of-snakes.html

Nonvenomous Snakes
www.kingsnake.com/hudspeth/Nonvenomous.htm

Python Snake
www.manbir-online.com/snakes/python.htm

Index